# ...AND L. A. IS BURNING

*Y York*

**BROADWAY PLAY PUBLISHING INC**
New York
www.broadwayplaypublishing.com
info@broadwayplaypublishing.com

Cover art by Andrew Ruthven, courtesy of Main Street
    Theater
First printing: July 2011
I S B N: 978-0-88145-505-2
Book design: Marie Donovan
Page make-up: Adobe Indesign
Typeface: Palatino
Printed and bound in the U S A

...AND L. A. IS BURNING was workshopped at the 2007 New Harmony Project (Paul Walsh, Artistic Director). The cast and creative contributor were:

HADDIE......................................................Susan Greenhill
SYLVIA ......................................................... Carrie Preston
ALVIN ...............................................David Alan Anderson

*Director*....................................................... Mark Lutwak

The premiere was at Main Street Theater (Rebecca Greene Udden, Artistic Director) in Houston, running from 11 October-9 November 2008. The cast and creative contributors were:

HADDIE..................................................... Michelle Britton
SYLVIA ...............................................Gwendolyn McLarty
ALVIN ...............................................................Timothy Eric

*Director*..............................................................Troy Scheid
*Set design*........................................................ Art Ornelas
*Lighting design*.................................................... Daniel Polk
*Costume design*...............................................Macy Perrone
*Properties design*.............................................. McKay Talley
*Stage manager*....................................................Rob Babbitt

The play was subsequently produced at Florida Studio Theater (Richard Hopkins, Artistic Director) in Sarasota, Florida. The cast and creative contributor were:

HADDIE......................................................Susan Greenhill
SYLVIA ......................................................... Celeste Ciulla
ALVIN ......................................Lelund Durond Thompson

*Director*...................................................... Kate Alexander

# CHARACTERS & SETTING

HADDIE, *white American, female, 45*
SYLVIA, *white American, female, 47*
ALVIN, *African American, male, 35*

*Place and Time: Seattle. April, 1992. A grocery store, an office, a TV station, an apartment.*

*No blackouts between scenes; it's all transparent, theatrical.*

*"..." is a hesitation, a breath, half a thought; a very little amount of time has passed, but there has been a shift.*

*"—" is an interruption, often by the next speaker, but sometimes the current one interrupting him/herself.*

for Korina Jones and Chris Jones

# ACT ONE

*(Scene 1. HADDIE introduces herself in Safeway. Nighttime)*

HADDIE: Those are overpriced.

SYLVIA: Pardon me.

HADDIE: Over priced. Get the ones in the plain bag.

SYLVIA: I don't like the ones in the plain bag.

HADDIE: They taste the same.

SYLVIA: I don't think they taste the same.

HADDIE: You get *more* and they're exactly the *same*.

SYLVIA: Excuse me, but they are not the same. *(With finality)* If you were to read the label you'd find out that they are not the same.

HADDIE: The label?

SYLVIA: ...The ingredients. The label. They are not the same. Sorbitol?

HADDIE: What's that?

SYLVIA: Exactly, what is sorbitol? That's the point. If I don't know what it is I shouldn't eat it. I don't want to eat it, I don't want my kids to eat it.

HADDIE: *(Triumphant)* You don't have kids.

SYLVIA: ...I beg your pardon?

HADDIE: No kids.

SYLVIA: ...How do you know that?

HADDIE: You're the writer, right? Sylvia Vanderlip.

SYLVIA: Are you following me?

HADDIE: I'm in 3-D.

SYLVIA: You're what?

HADDIE: 3-D. Apartment 3-D.

SYLVIA: Oh. Oh! You're my neighbor.

HADDIE: 3-D. Our balconies share a railing.

SYLVIA: Are you the smoker?

HADDIE: ...There's more than one smoker.

SYLVIA: Smoke comes into my apartment.

HADDIE: My method is to smoke on the balcony so it doesn't bother people.

SYLVIA: Your method might not be working.

HADDIE: My smoke bothers you?

SYLVIA: Somebody's smoke bothers me.

HADDIE: You know what bothers me? The kids in 4-D. At least I don't have kids—that would really bother you. I guess if you really had kids it would bother me, too.

SYLVIA: I was making a point about the kids. I was talking in shorthand. Trying to make a point about ingredients and how the cookies aren't the same. That's the only reason I mentioned the kids. That I don't have.

HADDIE: I thought shorthand was just for writing things down.

SYLVIA: When you're trying to make a fast point, shorthand is very convenient.

HADDIE: I'm trying to quit. That's why I'm here so late. Looking for crummy snacks to take my mind off smoking.

SYLVIA: Oh... *(Encouraging.)* Well, snacks, that's a good idea. Drinking water, keeping your hands busy. There's a lot of techniques. One of them is bound to work.

HADDIE: Yeah, then my smoke won't bother you.

SYLVIA: No, that's not what I—it's healthier if you quit. For you, I mean.

HADDIE: For you, too. Secondhand.

SYLVIA: I...I know it's hard, that's all...I used to smoke, it was hard to quit, but don't give up. They have support groups.

HADDIE: Did you use a support group?

SYLVIA: No, I...it was silly. It just happened to work.

HADDIE: I've tried a lot of stuff. Toothpicks, knitting. The patch is useless, except for how your heart races when you cheat, which feels *very good.*

SYLVIA: You mustn't cheat with the patch—you can die!

HADDIE: They don't know. They're guessing about half the stuff they say.

SYLVIA: They're not guessing about the patch can kill you if you cheat. They're right about that.

HADDIE: Like they were right about eggs? First it's no eggs, and then eggs are okay, but no red meat. Like I'm going to give up steaks and hamburgers. I never did stop eating eggs, and now I'm glad. Next thing you know *chocolate's* going to be good for you. "Sorbitol" will cure cancer.

SYLVIA: Sorbitol is not food. It's a chemical.

HADDIE: So's aspirin, but I'm supposed to take half a one every day. How is anybody supposed to make sense out of what they tell you?

SYLVIA: Talk to your doctor.

HADDIE: Yeah, who's that? I never see the same one twice. The last time I went and it was three years ago because of bronchitis and they made me go at my work, he wanted to do all these tests and procedures and pokes. He wants to stick a movie camera up you know where. Him and what army? He wants to know if I drink. I'm not there for drinking, why does he need to know if I'm drinking? Do I look like I'm drinking, is my hand shaking, are my eyes bloodshot? "One to two drinks a day is good for your heart. However, if there is a tendency to breast cancer in the family, any amount of drinking any time can *exasterbate* it." So drinking is good except when it's bad. I'm not going back for tests. They can keep their tests.

*(Pause)*

SYLVIA: *Exacerbate.*

HADDIE: What?

SYLVIA: You said something else. It's exacerbate—I'm sorry. It's a writer thing.

HADDIE: *(Earnest)* I'll write it down. Put it on a post-it by my desk so I don't forget. That's how I remember words. The Post-its.

SYLVIA: That's a...good system. I really should—

HADDIE: How did you quit if you didn't use the patch?

SYLVIA: Oh...really, it was silly.

HADDIE: Who cares if it works?

SYLVIA: I don't want to talk about it.

HADDIE: Don't you want me to quit?

SYLVIA: I—Kissing! They said kissing was the one surefire technique. Kissing—and, of course, I was a lot younger. I wouldn't now—

HADDIE: I don't think I can do that.

SYLVIA: No, no, of course not. You know, I really have to—

HADDIE: They make you go outside.

SYLVIA: ...To smoke?

HADDIE: Twenty feet away from the building. It's the only time some of those people talk. Otherwise they hate each other. Except when they're smoking. Then they hate everybody else.

SYLVIA: I have to get up at six o'clock—

HADDIE: Yeah, I go in early now, too. On account of job evaluations. I don't know why I bother. My unit partner is going to get the promotion. On account of affirmative action.

*(Pause. SYLVIA is suddenly interested.)*

SYLVIA: ...Your unit partner? Your Black unit partner?

HADDIE: Yeah.

SYLVIA: Affirmative action is for women, too —.

HADDIE: And if *I* get the promotion over him, he's going to say it's racist.

SYLVIA: He calls you racist?

HADDIE: Yeah. People sling that around the way they used to say *communist*. Now you're a racist, you can lose your job, lose your promotion. That's what I think.

SYLVIA: Do...other people at the office think that way?

HADDIE: Yeah, I'm not the only one. A lot of people think that.

SYLVIA: Um... *(Pause)* ...What was your name again?

HADDIE: I didn't say my name. My name is Haddie.

SYLVIA: Do you want to get together for coffee?

HADDIE: *(Exaltation)* What? You mean, like, get together? Have coffee?

SYLVIA: Yes.

HADDIE: Like to talk and all?

SYLVIA: Uh huh.

HADDIE: Get to know each other?

SYLVIA: Sure, why not?

HADDIE: They have coffee right here in the deli section—. Let's go—

SYLVIA: Tomorrow.

HADDIE: You want to come over to my apartment— 3-D?

SYLVIA: Oh, no. Why don't we meet here. At the deli counter.

HADDIE: Same time, same station. We'll have a nighttime coffee together.

***

*(Scene 2. HADDIE at work confronts an anonymous note.)*

HADDIE: *(to herself)* Oh, Man—

ALVIN: I'm going to get a coffee. Can I get you one?

HADDIE: *(to herself)* Shoot.

ALVIN: Can I take that as a "yes?"

HADDIE: No, you can't take it as a yes.

ALVIN: You want a drink of water or something?

HADDIE: Do I look thirsty?

ALVIN: You look like you're in shock. They give glasses of water for that.

HADDIE: Are you a doctor now?

ALVIN: I watch *Saint Elsewhere*. Glasses of water for shock.

(HADDIE *refers to a small pile of discarded Post-its.*)

HADDIE: Somebody put this in the middle of my desk.

ALVIN: Oh, yeah. You'll get a fine for sure.

HADDIE: A fine for what?

ALVIN: Littering.

HADDIE: Is this something new?

ALVIN: No—um—no. I was kidding.

HADDIE: I didn't dump it here. I shouldn't get the fine.

ALVIN: I was only kidding. There's no fine. What is it? What's the mess?

HADDIE: Garbage, Post-it garbage.

ALVIN: Maybe nobody put them there, maybe they just ...spilled.

HADDIE: *(Looking up)* From where? There's nothing up there.

ALVIN: It was probably an accident, don't be upset— somebody was dumping their trash can and some of it spilled on your desk.

HADDIE: There's a note.

ALVIN: ...Oh. Yeah.

HADDIE: It's not an accident when there's a note.

ALVIN: Can you tell who wrote it?

HADDIE: It's anonymous. It's an anonymous note. You can't tell who wrote an anonymous note. *(Reads)* "Do not put gummed paper in the recycle bin. Gummed material does not recycle."

ALVIN: It was probably just a joke.

HADDIE: It isn't funny that somebody thinks I suck on paper.

ALVIN: How do you get that?

HADDIE: Isn't that what gummed means—sucked on?

ALVIN: It's the glued edge. It's called gummed, it doesn't recycle... What's on the Post-its?

HADDIE: Are you accusing me of putting Post-its in the recycle?

ALVIN: No. I'm not accusing you. I thought we could find out whose they are by what they say. It would give us a clue.

HADDIE: What if they *are* mine? And they *aren't*, but what if they are? You still shouldn't put them on my desk with a note.

ALVIN: Why do you think it was me?

HADDIE: I don't mean you. I mean you somebody. Somebody shouldn't. I don't even use the recycle, I just throw my old paper away.

ALVIN: You're not supposed to—

HADDIE: I know I'm not supposed to. I know about recycle. But it's ridiculous.

ALVIN: The landfill is full—

HADDIE: No.

ALVIN: Yes. We're supposed to set an example—we're the Environmental Protection Agency.

HADDIE: It's a hoax. They're not making toilet paper out of it. The city is burning it for fuel at the power plant. They want us to pull out the paper so it's easier for them to throw it in the fire.

ALVIN: They don't burn it. We'd smell it if they burned it.

HADDIE: I was told they burn it...I read it. It's part of the electrical...electricity. They throw it in the electricity to make the power. I have my sources...I'm going on smoke break. (*She gets her coat and cigarettes.*)

ALVIN: I think I still have the memo about recycling—

HADDIE: I don't read memos.

ALVIN: ...I see.

HADDIE: You don't see, what do you see? I don't need a memo. I take notes at the meetings. Memos are for the people who don't pay attention at the meetings. I pay attention. I don't slough off.

ALVIN: You may be the only person in the room paying attention, Haddie. (*Pause. She is stopped in her tracks; stares at him.*) ...What?

HADDIE: (*Surprised*) You said my name.

ALVIN: ...I'm sorry, what?

HADDIE: Nobody ever says my name.

ALVIN: ...How do they get your attention?

HADDIE: They don't have to *get* my attention. I *pay* attention. My parents only ever said my name when I was in trouble. Harriett, is this your mess? Harriett, did you eat the rest of the cake? Harriett, dinner started at six. Harriett was a big fat cake-stealing mess-making late person. I made my aunt call me Haddie when I moved in with her. They shoulda said it nice. I like to hear it nice. ...You should pay attention at the meetings.

ALVIN: I'll try.

HADDIE: So you know what's going on.

ALVIN: I read the memos. Then I recycle them.

***

*(Scene 3.* HADDIE *pontificates over coffee at the Safeway.)*

HADDIE: He's always whining about how he's Black, how he can't get anything because he's Black. Let him try being a woman, see how far he gets being a woman. Soon as you're a woman you don't get any breaks. Not from the guy bosses not from the women bosses, the women bosses, they're worse. They want to keep you down to make out like they're really special because they got a supervisor job and you just didn't try hard enough, just didn't stay in school long enough.

SYLVIA: They say this to you?

HADDIE: I know what they're thinking. And notice how they're all pretty? Makes you wonder how they got their jobs.

SYLVIA: The female supervisors—?

HADDIE: Pretty, flirting, smart mouths on them, too. "Witty. My. Aren't they witty." I don't think she's witty. I don't know what they're laughing at half the time, and I don't care—tells me to recycle and then when I do leaves me anonymous notes.

SYLVIA: Who are you talking about—?

HADDIE: Let them laugh—she can't fire me— Ha! This is the government, and they can't fire you, and there's no cause to fire me because I work hard and sometimes more than eight hours.

SYLVIA: When you say "they" do you mean your female supervisor?

HADDIE: What?

SYLVIA: You're saying "they" and "she" and I wonder if these pronouns have the same antecedent noun. *(Brief pause.)* It's a pronoun-antecedent...thing.

HADDIE: *(Teaching.)* When I say *they* it's *they,* and when I say *she* it's *she.*

SYLVIA: Uh huh. And you think your supervisor slept her way into her job?

HADDIE: How could I know *that*?

SYLVIA: But you said—never mind... Do you get overtime?

HADDIE: It's the federal government. You don't get squat.

SYLVIA: I thought government jobs were the good ones. Like you said, it's hard to get fired. And you know as long as there is a government you'll get your paycheck.

HADDIE: *(Panic.)* What do you mean, as long as there's a government? Where is the government going?

SYLVIA: Nowhere. That's the point.

HADDIE: Then you shouldn't say it's going away.

SYLVIA: ...I'm interested in something you said...about how people use the term "racist" as they once indicted with the word "communist". *(Brief pause.)* Did your unit partner call you a racist?

HADDIE: *(Horror.)* Are you writing stuff down?

SYLVIA: Do you mind?

HADDIE: I thought you just wanted to be friends.

SYLVIA: *(Caught)* I'm a writer. We write things down. It's the dangerous thing about knowing a writer. We write things down.

HADDIE: In shorthand?

SYLVIA: Sometimes in shorthand.

HADDIE: Do you write novels?

SYLVIA: You don't know what I write?

HADDIE: No. The handyman said you're the writer. That's all I know.

SYLVIA: I write about economic disparity... *(Clarifying.)* Economic inequality. History. Basically non-fiction. Like that.

HADDIE: I like novels.

SYLVIA: ...What kind?

HADDIE: Short ones. So they're not so heavy at night. In bed.

SYLVIA: A standard criterion.

HADDIE: I dropped a book on my nose once. I was holding it like this and I fell asleep. Dropped it right on my nose.

SYLVIA: Must have hurt.

HADDIE: No, it was short. I think writers are interesting.

SYLVIA: That's because writers make writers the most interesting characters in their novels.

(SYLVIA *laughs,* HADDIE *doesn't.*)

SYLVIA: Just a little joke—in my experience, they're not that interesting. What does he say, your Black colleague, when he complains?

HADDIE: *(Surprised)* He doesn't complain.

SYLVIA: I thought...You said he complains that it's unfair, that promotions are unfair.

HADDIE: He *thinks* it...he doesn't say it. He thinks it. He'll say it, though. Once he's been in the office a little longer. He'll say it.

SYLVIA: I see. Did he grow up in Seattle?

HADDIE: I don't know.

SYLVIA: It's just that, some of the Black neighborhoods, they're pretty bad.

HADDIE: Dangerous.

SYLVIA: No, not dangerous, well, maybe. But rundown. Demoralized. High Point? It would be hard to make it on your own, coming out of a neighborhood like High Point.

HADDIE: I didn't have it easy.

SYLVIA: Have you been there?

HADDIE: No, but I know. You just have to pull yourself up.

SYLVIA: By the bootstraps?

HADDIE: Bootstraps. That's what I think, too.

SYLVIA: No, I don't— (Sighs.) There are some tough neighborhoods, that's all I'm saying.

HADDIE: I don't know where he grew up...What kind of novel are you writing?

SYLVIA: It's not...it's a non-fiction...novel.

HADDIE: What's it about?

SYLVIA: Pernicious systems—*hidden* systems. Race. America.

HADDIE: ...You ever notice how people don't listen?

SYLVIA: Oh, yes.

HADDIE: You listen. I think that's interesting.

(*After the briefest of pauses,* SYLVIA *puts away her notebook and stands to go.*)

SYLVIA: Well, goodness, thanks a lot. I have to go. I have things I need to prepare for work tomorrow.

HADDIE: You want to get coffee again tomorrow night?

SYLVIA: I'm busy tomorrow night. I think I have to work late. All week in fact.

HADDIE: Okay. I'll watch TV or something.

SYLVIA: Great.

HADDIE: I like to keep up with the trial. The LA cops trial.

SYLVIA: *(Brief pause.)* You're following the trial?

HADDIE: Yes, from the beginning. I'm fascinated.

SYLVIA: I'm...interested in it myself.

HADDIE: It's fascinating.

SYLVIA: You know, maybe we could get together after all.

HADDIE: You don't have to work late?

SYLVIA: I'll work late next week.

HADDIE: Okay. Same time, same station. Right here at the deli counter.

***

*(Scene 4.* HADDIE *does overtime.)*

ALVIN: How do you like my sign? *(Shows it)* "No gummed material." I'm putting it on the recycle bin.

HADDIE: Why are you showing it to me? I know that.

ALVIN: No, it's not for you, it's for the Post-it people— the ones who put Post-its in the recycle and the other ones who dump them on your desk...You going down? I'll hold the elevator.

HADDIE: I'm not going.

ALVIN: Five o'clock. Quitting time! Hallelujah, quitting time.

*(*HADDIE *looks at* ALVIN *blankly.)*

ALVIN: ...Sorry. Aren't you going home?

*(*HADDIE *shakes her head.)*

ALVIN: You okay?

HADDIE: Fine, I'm just fine.

(ALVIN *picks up the Superfund report she's working on.*)

ALVIN: I did one of these. January is me.

HADDIE: I did February. And *now*...I'm going to do February again.

ALVIN: ...Now? You mean right now?

HADDIE: Now.

ALVIN: It's five o'clock.

HADDIE: I heard you the first time.

ALVIN: I am Big Ben.

HADDIE: You're Alvin. And you're not that big.

ALVIN: No, you're right. I'm Alvin... Can't it wait? No offense, but when I get tired I make a lot of mistakes. End of the day?

HADDIE: I have to do it tonight so would you please stop talking to me so I can get finished. I have an important appointment. For coffee.

ALVIN: Nobody's going to read these until the beginning of next month. It can wait until tomorrow.

HADDIE: Except then I'll get demoted.

ALVIN: Nobody who can demote you reads them.

HADDIE: Somebody reads mine. Somebody reads everything I hand in—probably the same somebody who leaves me notes and garbage. And she's going to read this in the morning.

ALVIN: ...Aren't you guys, like friends?

HADDIE: Who?

ALVIN: You and Carol. The Carol who can demote us.

HADDIE: Why do you think that?

ALVIN: I see you out there smoking, laughing.

HADDIE: *(Amazed)* It looks like we're friends?

ALVIN: It does.

HADDIE: Oh. Well. *(A lie)* Yeah, we are. Smokers have a lot in common.

ALVIN: You should point out to her that you don't do your best work after hours.

HADDIE: Maybe I'll do that next time. I still have to do this tonight.

ALVIN: ...Do you have all the numbers?

HADDIE: In here. *(A folder)* What are you doing?

ALVIN: I'm really good at this. Move over. Do you know where you went off?

HADDIE: I mistyped the entries—you can't *do* this—

ALVIN: It'll go twice as fast. Read me the numbers.

HADDIE: It's not just correcting the numbers. I have to do the analysis at the end.

ALVIN: I'll do it in my head as we go along.

HADDIE: You have to show the calculation.

ALVIN: You can check it when I finish. Read.

HADDIE: Region One: Pierce County, American Lake Gardens/McChord Air Force Base.) AMOUNT: *(Very deliberate with her finger under each.)* 2 8 1 9 3.

ALVIN: Twenty-eight thousand, one hundred ninety-three.

HADDIE: Commencement Bay, Near-Shore/Tide Flats. Amount: 2 3 4 7...8. Are you staring at me?

ALVIN: ...No.

HADDIE: Because I don't like it when people stare.

ALVIN: No, no. Twenty-three thousand, four hundred seventy...eight. Just a sec. *(Regarding her errors)* Have you ever had your reading checked?

HADDIE: I can read.

ALVIN: For dyslexia.

HADDIE: I don't have that.

ALVIN: You transpose numbers. You could get tested.

HADDIE: I don't need to get tested.

ALVIN: Look at these mistakes. This isn't carelessness, you're mis-typing numbers because you're mis-seeing them.

HADDIE: Carelessness? Did Carol say I'm careless? Is that what she's saying about me now?

ALVIN: She's not saying anything about you—look at the numbers. Look at how you wrote them down.

HADDIE: ...She shouldn't rush me. I get very nervous. When I'm not rushed I'm fine, she won't let me type at a reasonable pace, she makes me hurry. I'm careful. (Demonstrates.) I hold up the page to the screen, I check every number, I know how to do this report, but she rushed me. What are you staring at?

ALVIN: No no, I'm not. That's a very good...method. Well, we won't rush. We'll go slow and we'll get all the numbers right.... Did you get dinner?

HADDIE: How could I get dinner?

ALVIN: I got half a Sub. I'll split it with you.

HADDIE: I'm not hungry.

ALVIN: Okay. Let me get a little bite though.

(ALVIN unwraps his sandwich. Brief pause)

HADDIE: Where did you grow up?

ALVIN: Saint Louis. East Saint Louis, actually.

HADDIE: Oh, you got a whole half left.

ALVIN: Yeah. I always get a foot-long when it's my free one.

HADDIE: I do, too. Eat it two days in a row.

ALVIN: Everybody does. So, you want some?

HADDIE: What kind?

ALVIN: Vegetarian.

HADDIE: Is that fish?

ALVIN: No... Vegetables. And cheese. Try it. It's pretty good.

HADDIE: Thanks...So, you didn't grow up in High Point.

ALVIN: Where's that?

HADDIE: In the Industrial District.

ALVIN: Should I check it out? I don't know any of the neighborhoods. I just got to town.

HADDIE: From Saint Louis.

ALVIN: Chicago. I was in the regional office in Chicago for a few years. I asked to be transferred.

HADDIE: Was it too cold in Chicago?

ALVIN: I needed a change. You know how it is. People get a notion about you, supervisors, they won't let you change even if you do change. You know what I mean?

HADDIE: *(Brief pause)* Yeah. *(Brief pause)* There's no reason for you to visit High Point.

ALVIN: Okay, I won't.

HADDIE: Visit the Space Needle. That's for new people. And tourists.

ALVIN: Yeah, I've been there.

HADDIE: *(Brief pause.)* When I was little I read the Esso sign as "three es es oh".

ALVIN: What's the "S O" sign?

HADDIE: The gas station! Before it was Exxon. I read the "E" backwards. Like it was a three. Is that dyslexic?

ALVIN: I think so.

HADDIE: What do they do for it?

ALVIN: I don't know, but they fix it.

HADDIE: Larry thought my reports were fine. Now Carol says I have to speed it up.

ALVIN: They're counting our keystrokes.

HADDIE: What does that mean?

ALVIN: Yeah, our computers are connected to personnel and they can see if we're playing Mine Sweeper or using electronic mail or track how fast we're typing in our data. Hello, Big Brother.

(HADDIE *inhales and exhales deeply.*)

HADDIE: I don't do that. I don't play Mine Sweeper. I don't know how.

ALVIN: ...Are you okay?

HADDIE: It's about not smoking. I'm breathing instead.

ALVIN: Eat some more of your sandwich.

HADDIE: Yeah, eating helps. Do you smoke?

ALVIN: I quit.

HADDIE: How did you do it?

ALVIN: It wasn't that big a deal—my father died of emphysema.

HADDIE: Your father *died*?

ALVIN: From emphysema.

HADDIE: My aunt died. Are you going to the funeral? Do you want me to cover for you?

ALVIN: This was years ago—years ago.

HADDIE: Oh. Then why are we talking about it?

ALVIN: It was from smoking.

HADDIE: Oh. Oh!

ALVIN: That's why I could quit. On his deathbed he was plugged into oxygen, wanted me to bring him a cigarette. I don't want that to happen to me. He was only forty-six.

HADDIE: That's young.

ALVIN: Yes. And getting closer every year.

HADDIE: How close?

ALVIN: I'm thirty-five.

HADDIE: My aunt had a heart attack. She took me to a play. Everybody was clapping and then she died.

ALVIN: I'm sorry.

HADDIE: It was *The King and I*. We both really loved it.

ALVIN: ...I saw that.

HADDIE: You weren't here yet.

ALVIN: It came through Chicago.

HADDIE: My aunt loved Yul Brenner.

*(Pause)*

ALVIN: *(Carefully)* He wasn't in it.

HADDIE: No. He was dead. But the new guy was great. We loved him.

ALVIN: So did I.

HADDIE: You know the part when the little Oriental girl gets chased by the dogs across the ice?

ALVIN: ...I do know that part.

HADDIE: It was really sad.

ALVIN: ...Yes. It was.

HADDIE: Then she died.

ALVIN: I thought she escaped.

HADDIE: She didn't escape. She died in the ambulance.

ALVIN: *(Trying to follow the illusive logic.)* Your *aunt* died in the ambulance.

HADDIE: That's what I said.

ALVIN: Not the little girl in the play.

HADDIE: No, she escaped.

ALVIN: *(Can't believe it)* Lord have mercy.

HADDIE: I don't like swearing.

ALVIN: I didn't—

HADDIE: We should get back to this Superfund report. I have an appointment.

ALVIN: Okay.

HADDIE: But... *(Inhale, exhale.)*

ALVIN: ...But what?

HADDIE: But it's very nice of you to help me. And I would like to thank you.

ALVIN: You're welcome.

HADDIE: And for the vegetables. "Municipal Landfill, Kent Highlands..."

***

*(Scene 5.* HADDIE *lectures about current events over coffee.)*

HADDIE: No, it's *good* that it's on the news every night—that way they can't pull any tricks. If they try to pull tricks everybody will hear about it.

SYLVIA: *(Writing notes.)* Which "they" is going to pull the tricks?

HADDIE: The district attorney's they.

SYLVIA: But isn't it the district attorney's *job* to prove that the cops are guilty—using whatever "tricks" at his disposal?

HADDIE: No. His job is to find out the truth.

SYLVIA: What is the truth?

HADDIE: The truth is that the cops are innocent until proven guilty.

SYLVIA: What does the tape tell us? Is the tape the truth?

HADDIE: It's not the whole truth. It's only part of the truth. They don't have the car chase. They don't have the part where he was escaping. The part where he was hurting the policeman.

SYLVIA: I believe there were *five*, five policemen. Do you think that has some relevance—some *importance*, the fact that he was outnumbered five to one?

HADDIE: We should hear all sides and then it's balanced. We should know what happened during the chase, and how scared the cops were. He was driving a big car and he could have killed somebody with it. The car was a weapon.

SYLVIA: What do you think would balance the tape?

HADDIE: The police job is to serve and to protect. They were serving and they were protecting somebody.

SYLVIA: Nobody else was there.

HADDIE: Maybe they were protecting each other.

SYLVIA: From the very first moment of the tape, he is subdued—he's subdued before they start beating him.

HADDIE: No, but see, the tape isn't the whole story. The tape...is the tip of the iceberg. It's an iceberg tip—a whole hidden iceberg of hidden information underneath the tip of the tape.

SYLVIA: What lies underneath? What do you think?

HADDIE: We don't know. The truth is under the water, but it could prove that the cops are innocent.

SYLVIA: *(Brief pause, closing her notebook.)* "The truth is under the water."

HADDIE: Are you done writing?

SYLVIA: Yes, I think I am quite done here.

HADDIE: Will you put in about the iceberg?

SYLVIA: I may mention an iceberg. An iceberg is a good idea. But not your iceberg, not the one where the cops are innocent.

HADDIE: What iceberg are you going to mention if it isn't my one?

SYLVIA: I'll mention the iceberg of hidden racism and lies. *(Grandly.)* "The American Iceberg."

HADDIE: What's the American iceberg?

SYLVIA: It could be a book title, reflecting four hundred years of White hate smashing into a human head.

HADDIE: Icebergs smash into boats.

SYLVIA: Don't you see? America is on trial here, not just LA.

HADDIE: LA isn't on trial. Just four policemen.

SYLVIA: It reverberates. All over the city, all over the country it reverberates. Suddenly all the claims of police brutality against Black people have to be reviewed with an eye to the likelihood that the police are lying bastards.

HADDIE: I don't like swearing.

SYLVIA: You know, I'm not surprised.

HADDIE: No, it's okay—just don't do it.

SYLVIA: I will sit here and bite my tongue.

HADDIE: We are supposed to wait until we hear all the evidence and then let the jury decide. The jury is the one hearing the whole iceberg. We just get what they show us on TV.

SYLVIA: Okay, let's wait. We will wait until we hear the whole iceberg and then lock up these rotten cops for life so they can be beaten and raped by their fellow jailmates—. (*Pause, appalled at herself*) God, I didn't mean that.

HADDIE: They could get AIDS if they get raped in jail. Do you want them to get AIDS?

SYLVIA: I just said I didn't mean it, I didn't mean it. All I mean is—you want the cops to be innocent until proven guilty, I want a few Black Americans to be innocent until proven guilty. That's all I want.

(*Brief pause*)

HADDIE: I like *The Cosby Show*.

SYLVIA: You what?

HADDIE: I like *those* people...I like Mrs Huxtable—how she is with the kids and how she says his name...Cliff... (*À la Mrs Huxtable.*) "Cliff?" You know the one about the fish?

SYLVIA: (*Packing up.*) I don't know the one about the fish.

HADDIE: It's really a good one—

SYLVIA: I don't watch TV like that. I watch TV—when I watch TV which I barely do—I watch TV to take the pulse of the country. If you want to know what people are being told to think you have to watch TV.

HADDIE: Rudy's beloved fish *died*...and they put on their dress-up funeral clothes—

SYLVIA: Really—I don't watch it.

(HADDIE *points at* SYLVIA.)

SYLVIA: What? What's wrong?

HADDIE: Are your clothes funeral clothes?

SYLVIA: No. They're work clothes.

HADDIE: They're very solemn. I thought maybe you had to go to a funeral.

SYLVIA: No. I don't know anybody here.

HADDIE: You know me. But I didn't die. I'm only forty-five. That's too young to die.

SYLVIA: Yes, it is.

HADDIE: Are you too young to die?

SYLVIA:—I don't know.

HADDIE: You don't know how old you are?

SYLVIA: Forty...seven.

HADDIE: *(Surprised)* You're older than me.

SYLVIA: I guess I am.

HADDIE: How come I look older?

SYLVIA: Well, I don't smoke for one thing.

HADDIE: Yes! —That's why I started, to look older. Now I gotta quit to look younger. *(She inhales and exhales with determination.)* It's your clothes. Your clothes make you look younger.

SYLVIA: ...You're right. It's my clothes.

HADDIE: Where do you get them?

SYLVIA: Nordstrom's.

HADDIE: I've never been in Nordstrom's. ...Don't you want to know where I get *my* clothes?

SYLVIA: Where do you get your clothes?

HADDIE: My aunt used to take me to Frederick and Nelson's. But it closed. And she died. Where is the suit section in Nordstrom's?

SYLVIA: Cosmopolitan Woman. Third floor. It's very nice. I'm sure you'll find something you like.

HADDIE: I get lost in department stores.

SYLVIA: They have signs.

HADDIE: Could you take me?

SYLVIA: Um...I—

HADDIE: I need to go soon.

SYLVIA: Um—

HADDIE: Tomorrow. Let's go tomorrow after my work.

\*\*\*

(Scene 6. HADDIE socializes at the office.)

HADDIE: (Proudly shows the report) Look. She said it's "thorough."

ALVIN: Thorough? That's all she said? It was *perfect*.

HADDIE: "Thorough" is good. She hasn't said anything nice about my reports since she took over the unit.

ALVIN: Did you talk to her? About not rushing you?

HADDIE: I don't talk to Carol about work. I keep it light. That's how come you see laughing out there in the smoking rain.

ALVIN: You should talk to her. She's doing your evaluation.

HADDIE: How do you know?

ALVIN: She's doing all of them. You want a good evaluation when promotions come up.

HADDIE: I won't get a promotion. I'm a seven-eight-nine. I'm already a nine.

ALVIN: You might get a promotion. They have to replace Larry. Carol can't keep running two units. Who better than you?

HADDIE: Or you! You might get it, too.

ALVIN: Yeah, I might. Did you hand in March yet?

HADDIE: I just finished it. I was going to ask you...

ALVIN: You want me to check the numbers?

HADDIE: Would you?

ALVIN: Sure. A promotion could be one report away.

HADDIE: Thanks. Thanks a lot. I work really hard.

ALVIN: ...Did you tell Carol I helped you? With February?

HADDIE: *(Smiling)* "Oh, that Alvin really helped me out."

ALVIN: *(Smiling)* We were a good team.

HADDIE: Yeah.

ALVIN: "Team work" is on the job evaluations.

HADDIE: And neatness.

ALVIN: "Considered a team player? Works well with others?" It's a whole category.

HADDIE: You get an "A" on team player.

ALVIN: It's not really an "A". It's zero through four. *(Pointedly)* Four's the best.

HADDIE: They can't really give anybody zero.

ALVIN: *(He knows all too well.)* Yes...They can.

HADDIE: I like "ABC" better. A is for Alvin...Alvin... *(À la Mrs Huxtable.)* "Alvin?"

*(Awkward pause.)*

ALVIN: I never really liked my name.

HADDIE: Were they always mad at you when they said it? Your parents?

ALVIN: No. They weren't mad. I thought it was a funny name. I didn't like it.

HADDIE: What, like the Chipmunks?

ALVIN: Who?

HADDIE: The Christmas Carol Chipmunks. The main one was Alvin.

ALVIN: ...I forgot about that Alvin. Yeah, that's a problem.

HADDIE: They were just on TV. A repeat. Did you see them?

ALVIN: I don't watch TV.

HADDIE: You don't watch TV?

ALVIN: That's exactly what I don't do with it. I don't watch it.

HADDIE: *Saint Elsewhere.*

ALVIN: What?

HADDIE: You said you watch *Saint Elsewhere.* They give you glasses of water for shock?

ALVIN: Uh, yeah, I used to...I don't watch any more.

HADDIE: Why do you have it?

ALVIN: ...For when my mother visits.

HADDIE: I like the news.

ALVIN: I like the newspaper for news.

HADDIE: I like to keep up with stuff that's happening. Around the country.

ALVIN: Uh huh.

HADDIE: In LA.

ALVIN: Movies?

HADDIE: No. The trial...I like to keep up with the trial.

ALVIN: *(With finality)* I'll wait for the verdict, thank you.

HADDIE: Well, there's not much doubt, do you think?

ALVIN: I haven't been following it.

HADDIE: The tape—

ALVIN: I haven't seen it.

HADDIE: You've seen it.

ALVIN: No.

HADDIE: It's been on TV a thousand times.

ALVIN: I don't watch TV.

HADDIE: *(She attempts to share some borrowed ideas.)* It's pretty clear. The cops beat the guy senseless... *Five* cops against one guy.

ALVIN: Then perhaps they will all go to jail.

HADDIE: Where they belong?

ALVIN: If they're guilty, that's where they belong.

HADDIE: We have to look at all the um...we have to look at the...um...it could mean the tip of the iceberg. The tip of the iceberg... "reverberates". Other Black people got lied about. About police beating them up.

ALVIN: I'm sorry? What?

HADDIE: Nobody believed them. The Black people.

ALVIN: *(Lost.)* Uh-huh.

HADDIE: The other Black people. Maybe they weren't lying.

ALVIN: I don't think I know who you're talking about.

HADDIE: Don't you think they're guilty? The police?

ALVIN: (*Let's put this topic to bed!*) I haven't been
following the trial. Damn. (*He has been nervously fiddling
with his cuff, has pulled off a button.*)

HADDIE: Why are you swearing at me?

ALVIN: I'm not—I seem to have pulled a button off my
jacket.

HADDIE: Oh. It's a nice jacket. You always look really
nice.

ALVIN: Thanks. My mother...

HADDIE: She takes you shopping?

ALVIN: My mother was fanatic about how we dressed.

HADDIE: Was she a clothes horse?

ALVIN: What's that?

HADDIE: Isn't that what it's called? Somebody who
wears a lot of fancy clothes?

ALVIN: (*Brief pause*) No. She is not a clothes horse. No
one in East St. Louis is a clothes horse. My mother tried
to protect us. She dressed us so the police could tell us
apart from the bad kids.

HADDIE: She believed in *bootstraps*.

ALVIN: She *believed*...that wrinkles were a direct line
to death is what she believed. We were neat, clean,
trimmed and ironed, me and my brother Sam. The only
ironed shirts on the street.

HADDIE: You pulled yourself up.

ALVIN: My mother did most of the pulling. And all of
the ironing and all of the *sewing*...I'll have to take this
to my tailor.

HADDIE: Did you get it at Nordstrom's?

ALVIN: I got it in New York on Orchard Street.
Everybody said if you want quality go to Orchard
Street. Jews are good tailors.

HADDIE: I didn't know that.

ALVIN: Yeah, my tailor here is Jewish. And if I ever
need a lawyer, he'll be Jewish, too.

HADDIE: *(Confused)* So he can sew your clothes?

ALVIN: No— ...It was a joke—you know, Jews, lawyers,
doctors?

*(Brief pause)*

HADDIE: I like *The Cosby Show*.

ALVIN: ...What?

HADDIE: On TV. *He's* a doctor.

ALVIN: Uh huh.

HADDIE: But not a Jewish one—he delivers babies.
*(Brief pause)* Do you like that show?

ALVIN: *(Rhetorical.)* Do I like Cosby? Are the cops
guilty? Do I like... basketball? Chitlins?

HADDIE: What are those?

ALVIN: Haddie— *(Breath, sigh)* Nothing, chitlins are
nothing...I haven't seen *The Cosby Show*. Okay?

HADDIE: But you know who Bill Cosby is.

ALVIN: Yes, I do.

HADDIE: Do you like him?

ALVIN: I like him.

HADDIE: I do, too...I know how to sew. You want me to
sew the button?

ALVIN: No thank you.

HADDIE: I'm trying to keep my hands busy. I may take
up sewing. Or knitting.

ALVIN: That's nice.

HADDIE: For the smoking.

ALVIN: That's good.

HADDIE: I'm trying different techniques. To quit.

ALVIN: How's it going?

HADDIE: Bad. Sometimes I get all the way into bed, and I haven't had a cigarette yet. Then I get up and light up. There's a technique I haven't tried. My friend recommended it, it's *surefire*. I'm might try it some day.

ALVIN: But you don't want to quit just yet.

HADDIE: I don't?

ALVIN: No. You want to keep having those friendly smoking sessions with our supervisor.

HADDIE: I do?

ALVIN: Until she writes up our evaluations.

HADDIE: Okay, just until evaluations are over.

*** 

(Scene 7. HADDIE *tries on new clothes.*)

HADDIE: Why are you looking over there?

SYLVIA: I am averting my eyes to give you some privacy.

HADDIE: Why do they have so many mirrors?

SYLVIA: So you can see yourself coming and going.

HADDIE: What do you think of this color?

SYLVIA: It's good.

HADDIE: Don't you think I should get black?

SYLVIA: Orange is the new black.

HADDIE: For slimming. She said black is very slimming. Do they always talk like that? "Black is very slimming," like I need slimming.

SYLVIA: In their eyes, we all need slimming. I don't think black is slimming. It's about the cut. Some cuts are slimming. Some cuts are bulking.

HADDIE: Your stuff's all black.

SYLVIA: I don't even know when it happened. I used to love red.

HADDIE: Maybe you did it for slimming reasons. I look like a pickup truck. You can see me coming and going a mile away.

SYLVIA: It's the cut. Try the A-line.

HADDIE: *(She does.)* Do you think she had on too much makeup?

SYLVIA: Who?

HADDIE: The saleslady. She had on a lot of makeup.

SYLVIA: I don't know. I didn't notice.

HADDIE: She looked like she was going to a party. False eyelashes.

SYLVIA: They all dress up.

HADDIE: All Black women dress up?

SYLVIA: No! All the *sales* women. It must be policy.

HADDIE: She talked down to us.

SYLVIA: She *was* a little odd.

HADDIE: Like she was talking to her grandmothers. Her *White* grandmothers.

SYLVIA: Maybe she was being polite.

HADDIE: Like we were deaf or something. *(Slowly)* "Come this way, dear." Like I'd never been here before.

SYLVIA: You haven't—

HADDIE: I know I haven't, but she doesn't know that. I think she talked down to me.

SYLVIA: She wouldn't. She wants you to buy something. She works on a commission.

HADDIE: How do you know?

SYLVIA: She came right up to us. She didn't wait for us to come looking for her.

HADDIE: No. She was letting us know.

SYLVIA: Letting us know what?

HADDIE: That she saw us. That we better not take anything.

SYLVIA: She thought we were going to shoplift?

HADDIE: What do you think of this one?

SYLVIA: She didn't think *I* was going to shoplift—

HADDIE: They're always on the lookout. I think this looks good.

SYLVIA: I would never shoplift.

HADDIE: The skirt— Do you like it?

SYLVIA: There, you see? It's the cut. Not the color... What are you doing?

HADDIE: I just want to see— *(Freeing her hair.)* Just a second. What do you think?

SYLVIA: ...I don't know.

HADDIE: Do I look younger?

SYLVIA: I'm not the person to ask.

HADDIE: I'm just asking for an opinion.

SYLVIA: Maybe get it cut. Shorter hair sometimes looks younger. Sassy.

HADDIE: I trim the dead ends.

SYLVIA: Something layered. And sassy.

HADDIE: Do you dye your hair?

SYLVIA: ...I have it rinsed. It lasts about six weeks.

HADDIE: There's a beauty shop in the strip down by us.

SYLVIA: Which one?

HADDIE: By Safeway.

SYLVIA: Oh. Don't go there.

HADDIE: Why not?

SYLVIA: I mean...They may not know how to deal
with your hair. Their clientele is Black... So they're
specialists... In Black hair.

HADDIE: Black hairdressers can't do my hair?

SYLVIA: Well, of course, they *can*. *(Getting tangled up in
her brain.)* But...why should you make them? If that's
not their specialty? And they might not even feel...
comfortable doing it.

HADDIE: Your hair always looks nice...Are you
married?

SYLVIA: I'm—no.

HADDIE: Divorced?

SYLVIA: Yes.

*(HADDIE expectantly awaits more information.)*

HADDIE: Well, I'm not going to tell anybody, for Pete's
sake.

SYLVIA: I'm divorced. I got divorced seven years ago.
We're still friends. I even like his wife.

HADDIE: Is she younger?

SYLVIA: It wasn't like that.

HADDIE: She isn't younger?

SYLVIA: Well, yes, she is younger, but she didn't happen while we were married. We got divorced. Then they got together.

HADDIE: *(Triumphant)* But he already knew her.

SYLVIA: How did you know that?

HADDIE: I read a romance like this. Do you have a boyfriend?

SYLVIA: I...I do, but he's not here. He's back east. In Boston.

HADDIE: When's he moving here?

SYLVIA: Why would he move here? I'm only here through June.

HADDIE: ...You didn't tell me that.

SYLVIA: Why would I tell you that?

HADDIE: Don't you think I want to know that my friend is only going to be here "through June?" Don't you think I want to know that? What if I get—what if I get...

SYLVIA: Invested?

HADDIE: What does that mean?

SYLVIA: You...um...get emotionally attached to someone. A friend.

HADDIE: Yeah, what if I get invested and you're back in Boston with all your other friends.

SYLVIA: I don't have friends in Boston, I don't have time for friends in Boston—I wasn't thinking is the only reason I didn't tell you. The year's almost up, so I just take it for granted everybody knows already. I wasn't thinking. Oh, god, deliver me!

HADDIE: Deliver you from what?

SYLVIA: Ohmygod, did I say that? ...Doesn't that
ever happen to you, you get caught in your mind
somewhere else, and you speak and you don't even
know it? *(Silence.)* I didn't mean to keep it secret from
you. It's no secret that I'm only here until the end of the
semester. I think I guess I thought I thought you knew.

HADDIE: Are you a teacher?

SYLVIA: I'm at the University. Through June. While I
research my book. It's a sabbatical from my regular job
at... In Boston.

HADDIE: Why do you live in the South End? Why don't
you live near the University?

SYLVIA: It's too...

HADDIE: Expensive.

SYLVIA: It's too White.

HADDIE: So what? You're White. I'd live up there if I
could afford it. It's not like the Black people are glad
we're in the South End. They'd just as soon have it to
themselves.

SYLVIA: Do you ever not say—?

HADDIE: What?

SYLVIA: No...Nothing. —That shirt looks good on you.

HADDIE: Does it make me look younger?

SYLVIA: It makes you look good.

HADDIE: Thanks. How can you tell if some guy likes
you?

SYLVIA: Oh, god, I don't know. *(She sits down.)*

HADDIE: Oh.

SYLVIA: What?

HADDIE: Look what your skirt did.

SYLVIA: It didn't do anything.

HADDIE: It rode up. It's very short when you sit down. That is too short.

SYLVIA: Says who?

HADDIE: It just is. We're too old for mini-skirts.

SYLVIA: Do you ever not say exactly what you're thinking?!

HADDIE: Why would I do *that*?

SYLVIA: ...No, you're right. You should. It's what I like about you.

HADDIE: You like me?

SYLVIA: I must like you—I brought you shoplifting—I mean—.

HADDIE: There are signs, right? How you tell when a guy likes you.

SYLVIA: I'm so not the person to ask.

HADDIE: How did you hook up with your boyfriend?

SYLVIA: He's fifty-eight. He can't be a boyfriend.

HADDIE: Did you ever have a younger-than-you boyfriend?

SYLVIA: Nothing serious.

HADDIE: But it's possible, isn't it?

SYLVIA: According to the popular media.

HADDIE: Yeah, it's not like the old days. How did you know when he liked you? The younger-than-you guy.

SYLVIA: ...We'd been on a panel together. We both stayed to talk to the audience. I asked if he wanted to get a coffee...

HADDIE: You asked?

SYLVIA: Yes.

HADDIE: You asked him?

SYLVIA: Yes.

HADDIE: Is that normal when you're older?

SYLVIA: I don't know—it's normal for me, okay? That's the way it's always been for me. Even my husband. I asked him first...did you ever hear that joke, "I know why he married her, but I can't figure out why he asked her for the first date."? That was me.

HADDIE: I don't get the joke—

SYLVIA: I knew I didn't have the usual...offerings. I stand more of a chance if they get to know me.

HADDIE: Then they fall in love with your mind.

SYLVIA: I don't know. I don't know if they actually fall in love with anything about me. Any of them.

HADDIE: Why do you say that?

SYLVIA: No, they don't. Real men aren't like Cliff Huxtable. Paul isn't in love with me. He doesn't come over. I have to drive over there...I mean...I mean he's always glad to see me, really glad, but I drive over there.

HADDIE: Is it far?

SYLVIA: It's Boston. Everything is far.

HADDIE: He should drive over sometimes. You should share.

SYLVIA: Well... He has more of a busy— no—that isn't true...but it's fine, really, we are incredibly fond of each other, and it's fine. We're not kids, you know, those days are over. (Pause) It's really very good.

HADDIE: It doesn't sound very good. He should fall in love with you.

SYLVIA: I mis-spoke. It's really very good.

HADDIE: I think there are signs that someone at my work likes me.

SYLVIA: What are they?

HADDIE: He stayed late to help me out.

SYLVIA: Could be he's just nice.

HADDIE: He stares.

SYLVIA: They all stare.

HADDIE: He shares his food.

SYLVIA: Okay.

HADDIE: He says my name. (*Pause*) You know. Haddie. He says "Haddie".

SYLVIA: I don't think that's a sign.

HADDIE: No, that's the best sign.

***

(*Scene 8.* HADDIE *shows off her outfit and hairdo at the office.*)

HADDIE: Did you check my March?

ALVIN: I did—look at you. You're all dressed up.

HADDIE: I dressed up.

ALVIN: What's the occasion?

HADDIE: No occasion.

ALVIN: Uh huh. Here's your report. It's perfect. All your numbers were correct and the analysis is smart. I added a little paragraph at the end. Or should I say, *we* added a little paragraph at the end.

HADDIE: You filled in the recommendation box?

ALVIN: A logical extension of our numbers.

HADDIE: But I never fill those in.

ALVIN: Sure, you do. February said, "Funds approaching end of March allocation."

HADDIE: I just say that so they know the region's going over-budget.

ALVIN: That's all I did.

HADDIE: *(Reads.)* "Recommend surplus funds be allocated to Fort Lewis, landfill number five." You told them what to do with the money. That is going to make them *mad*.

ALVIN: No, they'll be happy they don't have to figure it out themselves.

HADDIE: Why do you want the money to go there?

ALVIN: The families in the military housing are getting sick from the chemical fumes.

HADDIE: You think I should give it to Carol like that—with the recommendation?

ALVIN: Yes. She'll be very impressed.

HADDIE: I don't need to impress her. I had my evaluation this morning.

ALVIN: Oh, you had it. ...How did it go?

HADDIE: I told her how I need more time with the numbers. Remember? You said I should tell her? She said to take the time, she'd see how it goes. If it goes good, she'll tell the bean counters to stuff it.

ALVIN: I thought Carol was the bean counter.

HADDIE: No. The bean counters are in personnel. They sit there all day counting our keystrokes. Like you said.

ALVIN: What did she say? What did she say about your work?

HADDIE: I am much improved. I had an extremely nice evaluation.

ALVIN: Congratulations. What else did she say?

HADDIE: She likes my suit.

ALVIN: *(Trying to dismiss this topic)* Yes, it's very nice.

HADDIE: Nordstrom's.

ALVIN: Uh huh.

HADDIE: It wasn't on sale.

ALVIN: Too bad, but returns are easier that way.

HADDIE: I don't want to return it.

ALVIN: Then you're all set.

HADDIE: You think I should return it?

ALVIN: Not if you like it.

HADDIE: Do you like it?

ALVIN: It's nice.

HADDIE: But you don't like it.

ALVIN: I love the cut, and the color looks great on you.

HADDIE: It's the new black.

ALVIN: Uh huh. Did she say anything...about anything else? Carol.

HADDIE: She said my hair looks good.

ALVIN: Man, you two had a regular tea party in there.

HADDIE: No tea. She asked me where did I get it cut. Chantal's House of Beauty. My friend told me not to go there because they specialize in Black hair. But I went anyway.

ALVIN: You go to Chantal?

HADDIE: Yeah. You know her?

ALVIN: I go there, too.

HADDIE: You live in the South End?

ALVIN: In the condos with the boat dock.

HADDIE: I've seen them. By the park. You have a boat?

ALVIN: No. But maybe some day.

HADDIE: We live between MLK and Rainier. Where it's cheaper.

ALVIN: You and your husband?

HADDIE: I'm not married. You thought I was married? *I'm not married.*

ALVIN: You got a pet?

HADDIE: No—I want a pet. A lady invited me over for dinner after my aunt died. She has a cat. She talked to that cat more than she talked to me. If I had a cat I'd name her Sheila, after Sheila, Queen of the Jungle. I wouldn't talk to her more than I talked to my guest, though, but it would be nice to have a pet to talk to, when I didn't have a guest. I thought if I ever won Lotto, I'd buy a condo and have a cat. Maybe I should get a cat anyway, even if I don't have a condo. Or a fish. I'd like to get a fish, like that Cosby show? You know the one about the fish?

ALVIN: No—

HADDIE: The fish died and they had a whole funeral for it and everybody had to stand in a solemn row over the toilet in their dress-up funeral clothes.

ALVIN: I do not know the one about the fish.

HADDIE: A fish would be good company. Except one time I got home and there was a layer of ice in a water glass I'd left out. That would be bad for a fish.

ALVIN: It's pretty bad for people, too.

HADDIE: I just put on a sweater. Plug in the heating pad, get under the covers. Why did you ask me if I have a pet?

ALVIN: You said *we,* "we live between MLK and Rainier."

HADDIE: Me and my friend Sylvia. She lives in 3-C. I'm in 3-D. She's in 3-C right next door. She's a writer.

We're friends. She takes notes. She writes about the economic...world. She talks to me about smoking. A surefire technique.

ALVIN: So when you were talking to Carol? In your evaluation?...How were your numbers?

HADDIE: Up almost a point in every box.

ALVIN: I have mine tomorrow. My evaluation. First thing.

HADDIE: Don't worry about it. You'll do great.

ALVIN: I'll do great if she thinks I'm a team player.

HADDIE: She'll think that for sure. Everybody thinks that.

ALVIN: They didn't in Chicago...So, when you were talking to her, did you...did you....

HADDIE: What? Did I what?

ALVIN: ...Oh, man.

HADDIE: What?...Did I what?

ALVIN: ...Nothing...You want me to put this on Carol's desk for you?

HADDIE: Okay. Thanks a lot.

(ALVIN *exits with* HADDIE's *report.*)

HADDIE: (*Sings.*) Getting to know you. Getting to know all about you. Getting to like you, getting to hope you like me.

(ALVIN *returns. He is in shock.*)

HADDIE: What did you want to ask me?

ALVIN: LA is on fire.

HADDIE: Earthquake?

ALVIN: No. It's the verdict.

(*Intermission*)

# ACT TWO

*(Scene 9.* HADDIE *watches this on television, even though we don't see her.)*

SYLVIA: *(On a stool, wears a headset, talks into a TV camera.)* What did you expect, Ted? These are poor people without resources without power who have been the victims of injustice for four hundred years. They were anticipating a huge victory. Justice finally. This verdict wrenched the collective heart out of an entire segment of our country. Is it any wonder the riots are spreading—? San Francisco? Seattle? If the rioters are heartless, it is this verdict that has made them so. *(She holds the headset to her ear and listens.)* Not a *literal* victory, a *moral* victory to ameliorate a lifetime spent in an environmental wasteland, where the only new jobs are at the landfill, because they sure as hell aren't hiring at the power plant—these people don't get the jobs, they just get to breathe the exhaust fumes. And the rest of LA? the rest of white town, do they know, do they care? It's not just LA, LA is just the tip of the iceberg. The American Iceberg of silence and pernicious racism. White America doesn't have a clue. If it isn't happening on your street in your town, you simply haven't a clue. Here, here in Seattle, I live in a working class community, a community of desperately uninformed people who depend on what they hear on TV for all their information. One of my neighbors, working class, White, under-educated, desperately uninformed except for what *you* tell her, she is a study in bigotry—The first time I met her, she says to me, "people are screaming 'racist' the way they used to scream 'communist.'" I couldn't believe it—As if the two were comparable. *(Listens to her earpiece. Then, outrage)* Well, in the first place, Ted! When "people" were screaming communist, they were the people *in power*. The ruling class was screaming communist. When people scream racist, it's the powerless... *(Listens to earpiece)* Heal. I expect you to heal this nation, Ted. Heal the Haddies of the world. Show us the truth—the landscape. Show us where the money is, and where the garbage dumps are; where the good schools are, and where the liquor stores are zoned. Before you judge these rioters, look at the landscape. There are hundreds if not thousands of fires in South Central, but all the fire trucks are hustling over to Hollywood where the white people live. How can we fix this without looking at the basic inequalities. Where is your coverage about what is actually going on in this country? You're it, you're the only hope for information to get out there. The books are out there, I know they're out there, I write most of them. But nobody's going to the library, nobody's going to the bookstore except to buy their trashy romance novels. If it's not on TV nobody knows about it. Black America has known about the American Iceberg for four hundred years. Time for White America to catch up. Come on, Ted. You gotta help us catch up here.

***

*(Scene 10. HADDIE shows her apartment to her goldfish.)*

HADDIE: *(Entering with a goldfish in a plastic bag and books.)* See. This is where you're going to live, Sheila. I'll put you here by the window so you can look out. But not in the direct sunlight because then you could

boil. And if it gets too cold I'll put you on a heating
pad so you don't get frozen under an ice cap. You look
a little lonely in there. Maybe I should get you a friend.
But you know, you don't really need one because I'm
your friend. Okay? You like TV? I like *The Cosby Show*.
The Huxtables? They're funny. And they're Black, but
they're just like you and me. Only with more money.
And he's a doctor, so everybody goes to college. They
used to have a fish... *(Catches herself)* ...But never mind
about what happened to him. I'm going to get you
your own dish, one that blows bubbles into your water
so you can breathe. You can ride the bus to work with
me. Sit on my desk. Meet Alvin. You'll like him, he's
very handsome. And he's Black. We're not going to
watch TV today. We're going to read these books. I
have to return them in three days because the students
need them for their sociology classes. I can borrow
more books, too, the librarian said, as soon as I bring
these back I can get short ones that aren't so heavy.
That's what the lady was saying while you were in my
purse. I had to hide you because *No Pets Allowed in the
Library.* Except seeing-eye-dog pets. Sylvia Vanderlip
wrote these two books. She's in 3-C. One: *Inequalities
in American Schools: How the property tax is devastating
the public school system.* Two: *Environmental Justice in
America: The toxic poisoning of America's urban poor. (She
hefts it.)* This will really hurt if I drop it on my nose.

*(The doorbell rings.* HADDIE *gets quiet. A knocking)*

HADDIE: That's probably Sylvia Vanderlip now. She's
the writer. And she's our neighbor. And she's a fancy
TV person plus she's a sneak. If we are very quiet, she
will probably go away.

SYLVIA: *(Off)* Hello? Is anybody there?

*(A knocking.* HADDIE *doesn't answer the door.)*

\*\*\*

*(Scene 11.* HADDIE *isn't at the office when* SYLVIA *comes looking for her.)*

ALVIN: *(He is on the phone. With finality)* Mom, I am nowhere near the problem. I do not live in Capitol Hill, I do not work in Capitol Hill, I am not where anybody in Seattle was rioting, and it's over here anyway—the TV is just replaying the tape...I am sitting at my desk in beautiful downtown Seattle where everything and everybody is having a completely normal work day— Okay? You okay now? I gotta get back to work...I just talked to Sam, there's no fires, no rioting in St. Louis, you're fine, Mom... Do you see smoke in the sky?... Mom, that's not smoke, it's the dump smell. There is no fire...Mom. Go to the window and look outside. What's the sky look like?...See? You're fine...I'm at work, Mom, I can't do that...okay...

*(*SYLVIA *enters, unseen.)*

ALVIN: *(Sings.)* "Whenever I feel afraid, I hold my head erect and whistle a happy tune and no one will suspect—" *(He sees* SYLVIA.*)* Okaaay, Mom, now I really have to go. ...Soon. I'll take off a Friday next month and come home for a weekend. I love you, too. *(Hangs up)*

SYLVIA: Sorry.

ALVIN: Yes, ma'am. How can I help you?

SYLVIA: I'm looking for Haddie.

ALVIN: She's not in.

SYLVIA: Do you know where she is?

ALVIN: I'm sorry, I don't.

SYLVIA: Was she in yesterday?

ALVIN: ...Do you work in this building?

SYLVIA: No. I'm just looking for Haddie.

ALVIN: How did you get in?

SYLVIA: I walked in.

ALVIN: Did you show him ID or something?

SYLVIA: I just walked in. Took the elevator.

ALVIN: ...My god.

SYLVIA: What's wrong?

ALVIN: I had to show my ID, my driver's license and my social security card. Three days in a row— *(Laughs)* To the same guard.

SYLVIA: Let me guess? White guard?

ALVIN: ...As a matter of fact, no.

SYLVIA: You must complain. You must complain to his superior. He shouldn't treat you like that.

ALVIN: He's just doing his job. I don't want to get him fired.

SYLVIA: If he was just doing his job he would have checked my ID, too.

ALVIN: Then perhaps *you* should complain. You could demand equal harassment.

SYLVIA: People are idiots. This is not LA.

ALVIN: Right. No race problem here.

SYLVIA: Well, that is patently false.

ALVIN: ...I was being sarcastic. I'm sorry.

SYLVIA: ...I should have caught it.

ALVIN: No, I shouldn't have been sarcastic.

SYLVIA: No, it's all right. I'm from the East Coast.

ALVIN: *(Suppressing a laugh)* ...Uh huh.

SYLVIA: Are you Haddie's unit partner?

ALVIN: Yes, but she isn't in. Nobody's in. The only people in are me and Henry.

SYLVIA: Let me guess. Is he African American, too?

ALVIN: ...He is.

SYLVIA: All the people on the bus were African American.

ALVIN: All the people on the bus are always African American.

SYLVIA: I didn't want to bring my car downtown. ...Because of the parking. I wasn't worried about the car, or anything. I was worried about parking. I'm going to the rally at the court house.

ALVIN: I don't think you'll have any problem parking today.

SYLVIA: Are you going?

ALVIN: No, it's a work day for me.

SYLVIA: You said nobody is in.

ALVIN: The government is always in. Today Henry and I are the government.

SYLVIA: You should go. The mayor's going to be there.

ALVIN: Yeah?

SYLVIA: It will be very safe. A lot of police. A lot of security.

ALVIN: Oh, well, then it's sure to be safe—I'm sorry, I don't mean to be sarcastic, I can't help it. The mayor, the police? The government? Call in the National Guard? Uniformed men with guns? As far as I'm concerned, those are reasons to stay away.

SYLVIA: Seattle isn't like LA.

ALVIN: Yeah? Then what was Thursday night?

SYLVIA: Actually the riots on Capitol Hill didn't start until after midnight, so technically, it was Friday, the first of May. Our own little May Day. And that riot was a good riot.

ALVIN: And how is that, may I ask?

SYLVIA: Black and White people standing together.

ALVIN: And nobody ever gets hurt in an "integrated" riot.

SYLVIA: Well, of course, they do... Oh. You were being sarcastic.

ALVIN: Yeah...Sorry.

SYLVIA: ...Do you think Haddie's at home?

ALVIN: I do not know where Haddie is. Why are you looking for her? ...Are you her friend?

SYLVIA: No. I live in her apartment building. And I usually run into her. But I haven't seen her.

ALVIN: You're 3-C.

SYLVIA: I am.

ALVIN: But you're not her friend?

SYLVIA: No, of course not. I mean...I can't deal with people who are careless about pronoun-antecedent agreement.

ALVIN: Well. That narrows the field.

SYLVIA: I'm her neighbor. Her neighbor. When she comes in tell her Sylvia was by.

ALVIN: *That's* who you are. You were on TV. I saw you on TV. You preempted the final episode of *The Cosby Show*.

SYLVIA: I had no idea. On a normal evening, I'd have been watching it myself.

ALVIN: America needed a diversion from the violence.

SYLVIA: Glad to be of service.

ALVIN: No, you were not of service. America needed the Huxtables. You're a justifier. An enabler. Two wrongs don't make a right, ma'am. Even fifteen wrongs don't make a right. I'm not saying people don't have a reason or a hundred reasons or a thousand reasons to riot, and let me add, kill, I'm saying they don't have the right.

SYLVIA: Maybe *you* don't have the right. You have a government job with benefits. Probably a safe place to live, a car?

ALVIN: I *don't* have the right—no matter what I have or don't have or where I come from.

SYLVIA: And you're speaking for the Black community?

ALVIN: Oh, no, ma'am. I'm leaving that to you.

SYLVIA: ...Just tell her I was in.

ALVIN: She thinks you're her friend.

SYLVIA: Yeah? Well, she thinks you're her boyfriend.

ALVIN: No, she doesn't—what?

***

(Scene 12. HADDIE *has coffee at the grocery store deli.*)

HADDIE: (*Talking to Sheila in her plastic bag and sometimes blowing bubbles into the bag with a straw.*) This is a *Safeway*, Sheila. Safe Way. That's why it's open when nothing else is. It's the safe way. Other grocery stores are the danger way. I will get your dish for you as soon as the pet store opens, which I believe it will later this morning. Meanwhile don't worry about your air. (*Blows some bubbles.*) I got this food for you specially. It's large flake, and these are the ingredients: fish meal, dried yeast, ground brown rice, shrimp meal, wheat gluten, dried potato products, oat meal, soybean meal, soybean oil, fish oil, algae meal, sorbitol, lecithin, gelatin...Sorbitol. Whadayouknow...maybe they'll take it back.

SYLVIA: *(Entering)* I've been looking for you.

HADDIE: Aren't you done with me? You stole all my ideas, and now—

SYLVIA: Your what?

HADDIE: You stole them and put them on TV and now you just have to write them in your next book.

SYLVIA: ...Why didn't you answer your door?

HADDIE: I don't have to answer my door.

SYLVIA: You haven't been at work.

HADDIE: I went to the library. Sheila went with me.

SYLVIA: Who's Sheila?

HADDIE: My pet fish. I named her after Sheila, Queen of the Jungle.

SYLVIA: Sheena. Sheena, Queen of the Jungle.

HADDIE: Too late. I already ordered a dish with her name on it.

SYLVIA: What kind of dish?

HADDIE: For her to swim in!

SYLVIA: A bowl?

HADDIE: Yes, a bowl dish, but the pet store hasn't opened.

SYLVIA: People are still afraid. The stores will reopen when everybody feels safe.

HADDIE: The pet store isn't open because it doesn't ever open until ten AM. It's not from fear. Nobody's afraid. I'm not afraid. Are you afraid? Sheila is the one who should be afraid. She can't live forever in a plastic bag. Who's afraid?

SYLVIA: Everybody.

HADDIE: The lady behind the deli counter doesn't look afraid.

SYLVIA: She's Black.

HADDIE: Black people don't have to be afraid?

SYLVIA: They can be less afraid.

HADDIE: The only people who rioted here were White ones.

SYLVIA: No, there were White ones and Black ones.

HADDIE: *White* ones, and not in the South End either. In Capitol Hill. What does anybody make of that?

SYLVIA: I don't know.

HADDIE: Nothing about rioting rich White people in any of your books.

SYLVIA: You read my books?

HADDIE: Most of two of them. I get what you're saying, I get it. You're going to have to write a new book. About White people rioting.

SYLVIA: People are different here.

HADDIE: I never know who you're talking about. People this, people that.

SYLVIA: I never know who you're talking about either.

HADDIE: What do you want?

SYLVIA: Can't we just talk?

HADDIE: Are you going to write it down?

SYLVIA: No.

HADDIE: Get a fish if you want to talk.

SYLVIA: Haddie—

HADDIE: Don't say my name. You talked about me on TV. You said private things about me on TV. I can't go back to work—

SYLVIA: Nobody knows it was you.

HADDIE: You said my name.

SYLVIA: No, I didn't. I didn't. I wouldn't do that. I couldn't have. I'm positive I didn't say a name.

HADDIE: You never gave me a chance. You could have told me things and given me a chance. Instead you used me as your bad example on TV.

SYLVIA: What kind of chance?

HADDIE: A chance to change, but you didn't. You used me as *shorthand*.

SYLVIA: I was trying to make a point—

HADDIE: And you did, you made it. And now, you can go away. I have nothing more to say to you.

SYLVIA: You were anonymous. Nobody knows it was you. Except me. And I'm not going to tell.

HADDIE: You are not trustworthy.

SYLVIA: I'm sorry.

*(Pause)*

HADDIE: What did you say?

SYLVIA: I'm sorry, I'm so sorry.

*(Pause, this almost changes everything.)*

HADDIE: I don't know what I'm supposed to say.

SYLVIA: You could accept my apology.

HADDIE: ...I don't know how.

SYLVIA: Yes, you do.

HADDIE: I haven't...nobody ever apologized to me before.

SYLVIA: Say "I forgive you."

HADDIE: And then what?

SYLVIA: Then I'll feel better.

HADDIE: I mean...what do we do after I forgive you?
Are we supposed to be friends?

SYLVIA: Well. What people do, after an apology, is
sort of feel it out. Take it slowly. Test the waters. Go
carefully.

HADDIE: I guess you've done this a lot.

SYLVIA: I haven't.

HADDIE: Yes. Writing down what your friends say
and then telling it on TV, that would make for a lot of
apologies.

SYLVIA: We weren't really friends.

HADDIE: "Paul doesn't love me!"

SYLVIA: ...What?

HADDIE: You told me. Paul doesn't really love me, you
said that. You wouldn't say that unless I was your
friend. That's when I knew. You told me that personal
part.

SYLVIA: Paul doesn't really love me?

HADDIE: That's what you said.

SYLVIA: I've always wondered what was wrong. It's so
simple. Paul doesn't love me.

HADDIE: So what? You don't love him either.

SYLVIA: I love him. How can you say I don't love him?

HADDIE: Because you took a job in Seattle, and Paul
lives in Boston. Get a fish. They go with you any place.
You know the best part?

SYLVIA: I didn't know there was a best part.

HADDIE: I think I'm off cigarettes. They don't let you smoke in the library, and it took me so long to find the books...eventually my heart stopped racing. That's what your body does when it needs to smoke. It sends messages to you through your heartbeat.

SYLVIA: I know about the racing heart. Don't feel bad if you start again.

HADDIE: I'm not going to start again.

SYLVIA: It took me four tries to quit, is all I mean.

HADDIE: I thought the kissing was *surefire.*

SYLVIA: It was. It just took four tries.

HADDIE: I'm quitting this first time. I don't need four tries.

SYLVIA: Yeah, okay, you're quitting this time. I'm really sorry. I thought I could use what you said and how you felt to make a point. I didn't think it would hurt you.

HADDIE: You didn't care if you hurt me.

SYLVIA: Then why am I here?

HADDIE: So you can feel better. I'll think about it. But right now, I have to say, I don't think so. I have to go return this fish food.

(HADDIE *exits with Sheila.* SYLVIA *sits there.*)

*** 

(*Scene 13.* HADDIE *shows Sheila, in her new bowl, the cubicle.*)

HADDIE: This is our cubicle. That's my computer.

(ALVIN *enters.*)

ALVIN: Didn't you tell Carol I helped you with your reports?

HADDIE: This is Alvin. This is Sheila. This is her dish. This is her food, zooplankton, it's organic, right there in Safeway. Isn't she pretty?

ALVIN: We aren't allowed to have pets.

HADDIE: People have flowers.

ALVIN: It's not the same.

HADDIE: Flowers cause sneezes. Fish cause joy.

ALVIN: She'll die over some weekend.

HADDIE: She's going back and forth with me on the bus. Until winter. Then she'll stay home on the heating pad. In her dish.

*(Brief pause)*

ALVIN: I thought you told Carol I helped you with the reports.

HADDIE: I didn't.

ALVIN: Well, that explains it anyway.

HADDIE: Was I supposed to? I didn't know you wanted me to.

ALVIN: I wanted you to.

HADDIE: Why didn't you ask me to?

ALVIN: I thought you could figure it out. She gave me a Two.

HADDIE: A Two?

ALVIN: On team work.

HADDIE: Oh! Don't worry, they won't give the promotion to me. They have to give it to you.

ALVIN: No, they don't. They're bringing in somebody else. They're bringing in a guy from LA.

HADDIE: Is he Black?

ALVIN: How would I know that?

HADDIE: The Black people will want to transfer out of
LA.

ALVIN: Yeah, all of them in one fell swoop. A gigantic
transfer to the open and friendly Pacific Northwest
corner of America.

HADDIE: Except here White people riot.

ALVIN: ...Your friend was here.

HADDIE: What friend? Sheila?

ALVIN: I forget her name.

HADDIE: Sheila's my fish.

ALVIN: Your other friend. Your friend in 3-C.

HADDIE: *(Worried.)* Oh, no. What did she say?

ALVIN: She was rallying behind the rioters.

HADDIE: Did she say anything about me?!

ALVIN: Your pronouns need work.

HADDIE: ...I don't think like that anymore.

ALVIN: Like what?

HADDIE: *Communism*? I thought like that *before*, but I
read the book—

ALVIN: *(Sarcasm.)* Oh, you read a book.

HADDIE: And I went to High Point—I wanted to see
it— And I don't think like that now. She shouldn't
have said those things on TV. She didn't give me a
chance. I don't think like that—oh man. *(She looks for a
cigarette.)* Do you have...no, you don't smoke. She is not
right about me. I'm not like that any more.

ALVIN: She's not right about anything.

HADDIE: She doesn't know anything about me. I have
will power I'm quitting. *(She inhales and exhales with
purpose.)*

ALVIN: What's wrong with you?

HADDIE: I don't want to smoke.

ALVIN: Then don't.

(HADDIE *has an epiphany.*)

HADDIE: Oh, my god. Could you do me a favor?

ALVIN: Why not, why not do you a favor...sure, Alvin is a team player, he always does you a favor.

HADDIE: I'm trying to quit.

ALVIN: Let old Alvin help you out. What? I should fetch you coffee and a bun from the snack wagon?!

HADDIE: No, no. Just stand there. Don't move. Close your eyes.

ALVIN: Holy Mother, give me patience.

HADDIE: And don't swear, please.

(ALVIN *stands, eyes closed. She takes a big breath, exhales, then kisses him gently on the mouth.*)

ALVIN: Oh god, oh my god, woman, what, what now?

HADDIE: To quit smoking. It's surefire.

ALVIN: Are you out of your mind?

HADDIE: I think it helped.

ALVIN: I am not your boyfriend—

HADDIE: But you like me.

ALVIN: I like you?

HADDIE: You gave me your sandwich. You told me about your father—he died, and your mother ironed your shirt.

ALVIN: What would it have cost you? You knew you weren't going to get the promotion, you said so, you're a seven-eight-nine, they practically have to get an act of Congress to give you *a raise*—

HADDIE: No, they don't—

ALVIN: What would it have cost you to toss it my way? You know I'd take care of you if I was your boss.

HADDIE: I didn't know you wanted to be my boss. How could I know that? Why didn't you ask me?

ALVIN: Because I'd rather die than ask you for anything.

*(Pause)*

HADDIE: I didn't know you wanted Larry's job.

ALVIN: What did you think? Staying late to help you out, redoing your reports, what did you think? I wanted a date—? I wanted to date you? Date you? Is that what you thought, the office Black Man wants to date you? You? —You stupid Whitewoman!

*(Pause. A tremendous amount of damage has just been done. HADDIE straightens her desk, doesn't look up.)*

ALVIN: *(Mocking.)* "But you like me."

*(Pause. HADDIE begins to fall apart.)*

HADDIE: She should have given you a four. I should have—

ALVIN: Yeah, you should have—

*(HADDIE gets a big book out of her bag.)*

HADDIE: *(Numb.)* Why didn't I know this, I should know this. The power plants, the sewage, the landfills are always where the poor people live. There's no landfill in Capitol Hill.

ALVIN: There certainly isn't.

HADDIE: I went to High Point, the sewage treatment plant...it smells so bad...right by the school. The kids came over to me, why aren't you in school, does it always smell like this? Take us for a ride, take us for a ride. I can't take you for a ride, your parents will get really mad...it always smells, always, and I better go home...go home...go away...they were all so neat and clean and ironed, but the street and the smell, I can't forget the smell. I should have said you were a four—

ALVIN: It's over. It's over. Forget it, just forget it—

HADDIE: How can they learn with that smell, that horrible smell, in the halls in the classrooms—

(ALVIN *is listening now, hearing.*)

HADDIE: I can't get it out of my nose. You can't pick yourself up out of that smell. It doesn't matter if your mother irons your shirt or pulls on your boots. I don't know how you can learn with that smell.

ALVIN: ...You can't learn with that smell. You can't.

(*Brief pause. Sorrow in the room.*)

HADDIE: I'm so stupid.

ALVIN: (*Brief pause*) I'm sorry. I'm sorry, Haddie.

HADDIE: I should have...but now...there's too much I don't know...I'll never be able to catch up...I can't catch up...I'm so stupid—I can't catch up—

ALVIN: You're doing fine. You'll catch up.

HADDIE: I have to go out. I need—I need— (*She finds cigarettes.*)

ALVIN: Put those down, you're quitting.

HADDIE: I know it isn't break time, I won't go later I'll go now...I need...I need....I need to...I get four tries, four tries to quit...

(ALVIN *kisses her, hard and fast. Silence as they look at each other, both amazed, in shock.*)

ALVIN: (*With slow determination*) Haddie? Haddie? You know, you know the one about the fish? The episode about the fish? The one where they get dressed up and go into the bathroom and pray and flush the fish? It's a great one, that one. When I buried my Dad, that's what I thought of, the time when we all sat in the living room laughing our guts out over that poor dead fish. I love *The Cosby Show*, Haddie. I loved it when we all sat down to watch the Huxtables, listening to that family say stuff we didn't know how to say to each other, and for half an hour all the bad stuff just went away, you know that? Do you know that, Haddie?

HADDIE: *(She nods.)*

ALVIN: Don't smoke. Okay?

HADDIE: *(She nods.)*

ALVIN: This from a friend. Your *friend* Alvin doesn't want you to smoke. *(Brief silence.)* Okay?

*(HADDIE nods.)*

ALVIN: I'm sorry, Haddie. Okay?

HADDIE: You are?

ALVIN: Really sorry.

HADDIE: ...And now I have to...We have to..we take it slowly? We test the waters?

ALVIN: Yeah. We'll test the waters.

HADDIE: Okay.

ALVIN: *(He tries to take them to higher ground.)* Give me those. *(He rips up her cigarettes.)* These are bad for you. Make you die young, these do. Take off your coat. Sit down. Let me see...um. Let's do April. What do you say, should we do April?

HADDIE: April?

ALVIN: Yeah. The April report. We'll do it together.

HADDIE: April.

ALVIN: Yeah, from the beginning. We'll get it right the first time this time. So...what do you think about April?

HADDIE: I talked to Sheila about April.

ALVIN: Sheila your fish?

HADDIE: Uh huh.

ALVIN: And what did the two of you decide about April?

HADDIE: We were talking yesterday about April. I told Sheila, we could...in the box...?

ALVIN: What box?

HADDIE: In the box at the end of the report?

ALVIN: *(Nodding)* Uh-huh.

HADDIE: We could make a recommendation. If we were to see some problems...like the bad smell near the school. We could make some recommendations about the money.

ALVIN: Tell them where to allocate their money?

HADDIE: Can we do that? Tell our new boss? Can we do that?

ALVIN: Yes. We can do that. We'll do it together.

HADDIE: Make a recommendation.

ALVIN: Yes, we will make a recommendation to the new boss. From Haddie and Alvin.

HADDIE: From Haddie and Alvin.

*(The lights stay on. But the play ends here.)*